MAKING POP-UP GREETING CARDS

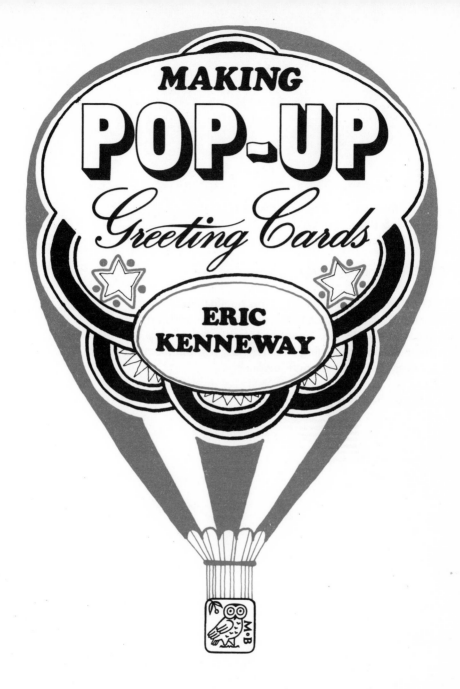

MAKING POP-UP
Greeting Cards

ERIC KENNEWAY

Mills & Boon Limited, London

First published 1972 in Great Britain
by Mills & Boon Limited
17–19 Foley Street, London W1A 1DR

ISBN 0 263.05065.3

Made and printed in Great Britain by
Butler & Tanner Ltd, Frome and London

Contents

Introduction

Whenever we open a pop-up card there is a moment of magic as it comes to life in our hands. Pop-up cards are fun to receive and even more fun to make. This book will show you how to make cards with many different actions together with other greeting novelties. By following the step-by-step instructions you will be able to make each type of card and then to use the techniques you have learnt immediately to construct cards of your own design. You will also be able to assemble a pop-up book in which to keep samples of your work.

Teachers will find that pop-up card making need not be simply an isolated end-of-term activity in preparation for Christmas or Easter. It can be employed throughout the year as a light-hearted and enjoyable craft which will help to develop useful skills. The equipment and materials needed are to be found in every classroom.

MATERIALS

To make the cards in this book you will need paper, something to cut with and something to draw with. For some you will also need a ruler and glue.

Paper should be strong without being thick. Most ordinary drawing papers are suitable. A quarter imperial sheet (11" × 15") makes a card of reasonable size.

Scissors are adequate for cutting, but if possible it is better to use a craft knife with blades which can be replaced. When cutting with a knife, it may be necessary to protect your work surface with a wooden board or cardboard.

A pencil symbol is used in the diagrams to indicate lines which are drawn and it is advisable to use a pencil first so that construction lines can be rubbed out. But of course it is quite permissible to use paints, crayons and coloured inks as well. In some cases you may want to incorporate cut out paper shapes or pieces of fabric into your designs.

HOW TO USE THIS BOOK

If you like you can start by picking out a card which attracts you from
any part of the book and make it straightaway from the diagrams. But
it really is better to start at the beginning and familiarise yourself with
the simpler techniques first. In this way you will gain a better
understanding of what makes pop-up cards pop and you will be better
armed when you come to explore the possibilities of developing your
own ideas.

But either way, there are some general rules or principles that you
should take note of first.

NOTES ON TREATMENT

Many of the actions are dependent on the crease lines being firm and
accurate. Always fold as neatly as possible and try to avoid accidental
or misplaced creases. If you do have a crease in your card which is
spoiling the action, or an unwanted cut, you may be able to correct it
by sticking a strip of gummed paper to the reverse side. It will not be
visible when the card is finished because it will lie hidden between two
layers of paper.

Your cards will have a better finish if you always glue the edges of the
two layers together at the end.

Some pop-up cards are purely decorative. Others – often humorous
ones – tell a 'story', so they should have a beginning, a middle and an
end.

The front of the card should be used for the beginning of the story. It
should prepare us for what is to come inside. As a general rule, the
middle of the story is the pop-up action and the end is the text which
accompanies the action and which sums up or clarifies what has gone
before.

This may more easily be understood after looking at the illustration of
a card of this type. The phrase, COME BACK . . . prepares us so that
when the card is opened we easily 'read' the woman's action of
opening her arms as a welcoming gesture. Then our eyes move on to
the final explanatory phrase, ALL IS FORGIVEN.

The way in which the front of a pop-up card is decorated is important for another reason. What you write or draw there must indicate clearly which way is the right way up. If an ambiguous design without lettering is used, the card may be opened upside down unwittingly and if this is done the effect of the card will be spoiled.

Symbols

The following symbols are used throughout:

A coloured line is a line to be drawn.

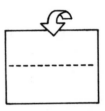

A line of dashes should be folded into a concave crease (valley fold).

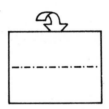

A line of dots and dashes should be folded into a convex crease (mountain fold).

Faint black lines represent existing creases.

A heavy black line is a line to be cut.

Opening flowers

First of all you will discover how to make a card with a flower inside which opens when the card is opened. You can equally well use a smiling sun as an alternative design.

When you have made one of these, study how the action works and try to apply this same action to your own design ideas. The designs you choose should have some relevance to the opening and expanding action that this type of card has. There would be little point in drawing a house, for example, but it might be possible to adapt the human figure to this action and make a man do physical jerks.

If you want to experiment with asymmetrical shapes, you can omit steps 2—4, and instead, make a complete drawing in the upper rectangle centred where the diagonal creases cross. Then you should cut around the outline at top and bottom, taking care not to cut beyond the diagonal creases.

Minimum materials needed

paper/pencil/knife or scissors

OPENING FLOWER

1. Fold the top and bottom edges of your paper together. Crease firmly and open. Make diagonal creases in the lower rectangle.

2. Fold the left edge behind to the right edge.

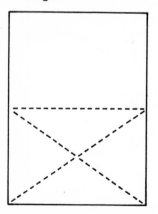
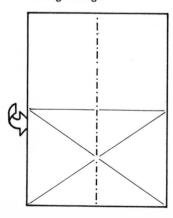

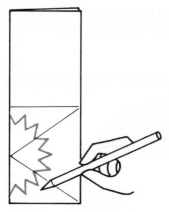

3. Draw the right half of a flower or some other design, centred where the diagonal creases meet.

4. Cut around your design from the folded edge to the diagonal creases only. Open up.

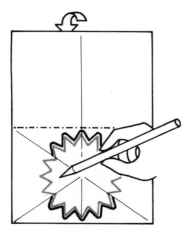

5. Complete your design. Then fold the top edge behind to the bottom edge.

6. Close the card from left to right, allowing the cut edges of your design to project forward by folding along the lines as shown.

7. Finally, decorate the front of the card.

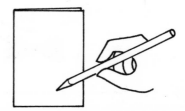

WINKS and SMILES

On the following pages you will find instructions for making cards with faces which smile or close one eye in a wink.

Wink and smile actions may be used with straightforward happy faces of seasonal figures such as Father Christmas or clowns. They can also be used to add point to a message or give it a double meaning. When a message is accompanied by a broadly winking face, its meaning may be quite altered.

Mouths of animals as well as humans, and particularly the beaks of birds, can be constructed in the same way as the winking eye.

Minimum materials needed

paper/pencil/knife or scissors

WINK

1. Fold the top and bottom edges together. Crease firmly. Open and fold left edge to right edge.

2. Make a short horizontal cut from the folded edge at some point below the halfway crease.

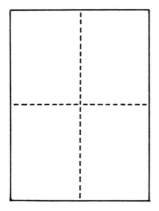

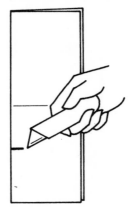

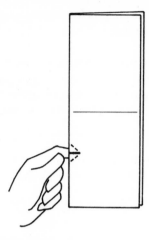

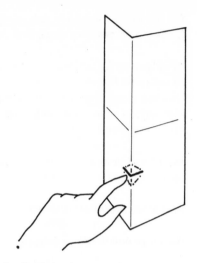

3. Fold the edges of the cut just made backwards and forwards once or twice to make good creases. Notice that the angle of these folds is somewhat less than 45 degrees from the horizontal. Unfold.

4. Push in the cut edges so that they project behind.

5. Press firmly and open.

6. Now draw your design. Fold the top edge behind to the bottom edge.

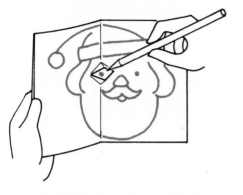

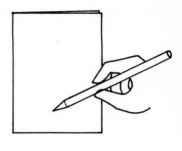

7. Partly close the card so that the 'eyelids' project forward. Now you can draw the pupil of the eye on the under layer of paper.

8. Finally, decorate the front of the card.

SMILE

First, fold the top and bottom edges of a rectangle of paper together. Make a crease and open up. Fold the left edge to the right edge.

1. Make a slanting cut from the folded edge at some point well below the centre horizontal crease.

2. Fold the lower edge of the cut just made backwards and forwards to make a firm crease.

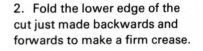

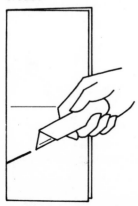

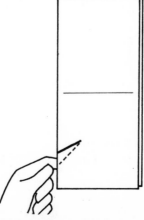

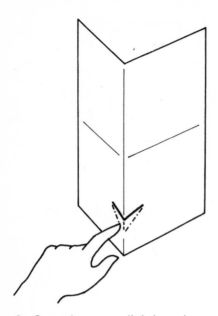

3. Open the paper slightly and push the lower 'lip' in.

4. Close and press firmly. Open up.

6. Close the card from left to right.

5. Fold the top edge behind to the bottom edge. Draw a face around the cut mouth.

7. Finally, decorate the front of the card.

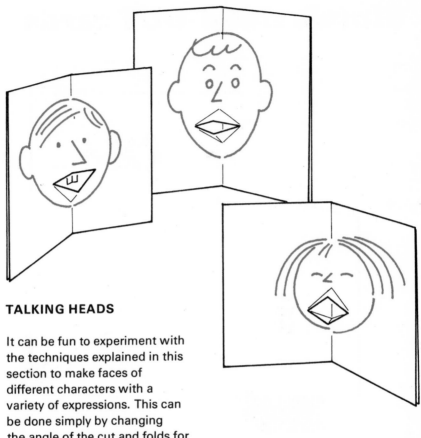

TALKING HEADS

It can be fun to experiment with
the techniques explained in this
section to make faces of
different characters with a
variety of expressions. This can
be done simply by changing
the angle of the cut and folds for
the mouth. First make the
mouth and then decide what
sort of face will match it. Try
making a set of characters from
post cards. You can make them
'talk' by holding the side edges
between thumb and forefinger
and alternately squeezing and
opening.

Simple *stand-OUT* cards

All the cards shown in the accompanying illustration have a simple three-dimensional effect. Instructions follow for making the card with a stand-out Christmas tree, but the angel is made in exactly the same way. In fact, almost any subject can be adapted, but whatever design you choose, while making your drawing you should bear in mind where the cuts are to be made subsequently.

The ship is made in a slightly different way from the others. It has four straight horizontal cuts, the widest at the bottom and the narrowest at the top. Such a card might be used to wish someone, BON VOYAGE.

As well as making the cross cuts which allow the design to stand out, additional cuts can be made within the design purely for their decorative effect.

Minimum materials needed

paper/pencil/ruler/knife or scissors

STAND-OUT CHRISTMAS TREE

1. Find the centre lines by folding the sides together in turn, making creases and opening up. Call the vertical line *A*.

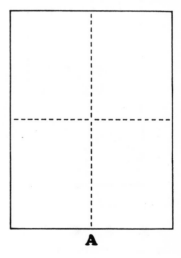

A

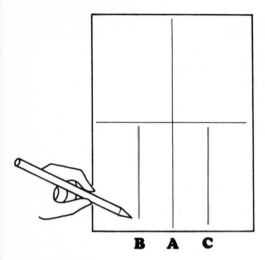

B   A   C

B   A   C

2. In the lower half, draw equidistant vertical lines on either side of line *A*. Call these lines *B* and *C*. $AB = AC$.

3. Fill the space between lines *B* and *C* with your design.

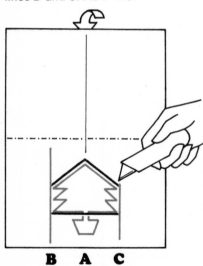

B   A   C

5. Close from left to right, allowing the design to project forward.

4. Cut above and below your design from line *B* to line *C* or, as here, allow one of your cuts to pass through the design where suitable.

Fold top edge behind to bottom edge.

6. Finally, decorate the front of the card.

More complex stand-OUT cards

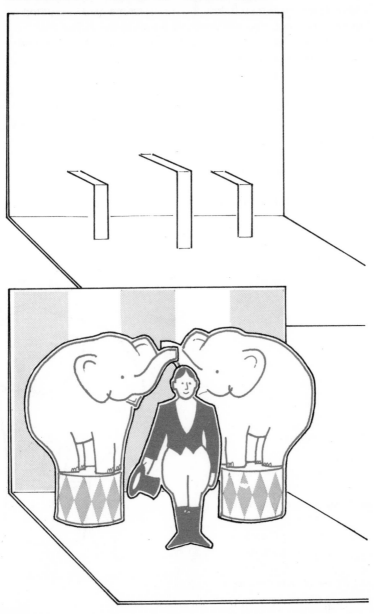

This section is concerned with making two more types of card which have a three-dimensional effect.

The first type has several support strips to which cut out shapes can be glued. The instructions which follow are for making a card illustrated with a bunch of flowers. You will probably find it easier to use the same technique to construct scenes such as the circus which is made up of free-standing figures. Pictures cut from magazines can be employed in this type of scene.

The second type is a flat-fronted stand-out card which is a way of making three-dimensional versions of box-like subjects such as houses, cars and so on.

Minimum materials needed

paper/pencil/ruler/knife or scissors/glue

Glue is not needed for the flat-fronted stand-out card.

3–D CIRCUS SCENE

A card such as this can be made by following the instructions for the vase of flowers, except that in step 2, the central pair of cuts should be made to line *C* and the other two pairs of cuts to line *B*. Of course, the number of support strips does not have to be limited to three.

STAND–OUT VASE OF FLOWERS

First make the centre crease by folding in half widthways. Then fold the left-hand edge forward to the centre crease.

1. Draw three vertical lines *A, B* and *C* on the upper flap. It is important that *C* be placed no further to the right than halfway between the folded edge and the centre crease.

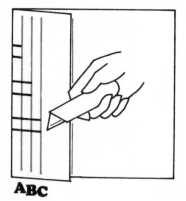

ABC

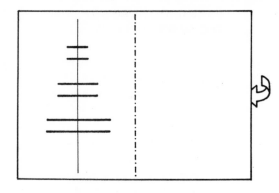

2. Make pairs of cuts from the folded edge to lines *A, B* and *C* in turn. Open up.

3. Fold the right-hand edge behind to the left-hand edge.

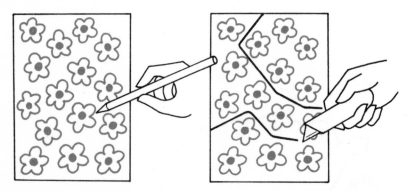

4. On a separate sheet of paper, about half the size of your first sheet or even less, draw a mass of flowers. Make them quite large and simple.

5. Now cut this sheet into three fairly arbitrary sections.

6. Trim any surplus paper from
your three sections of flowers.

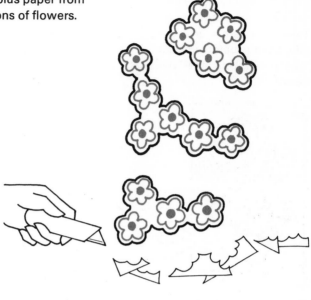

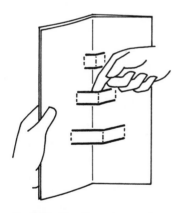

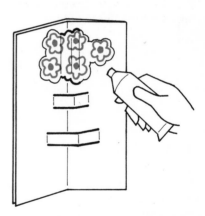

7. Take the first sheet of paper
and pull the three strips forward
one at a time. Make firm
creases.

8. Now stick one of the flower
sections to the topmost strip,
after creasing it to match the
change of angle in the strip.

Next stick another flower section
to the middle strip, if possible
arranging it so that it partly
overlaps the first one.

Stick the remaining flower
section to the bottom strip.
Take some care in arranging
your flowers before sticking
them down. Unwanted ones can
be cut off.

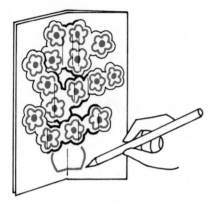 

9. Complete your design. Close
the card from left to right.

10. Finally decorate the front of
the card.

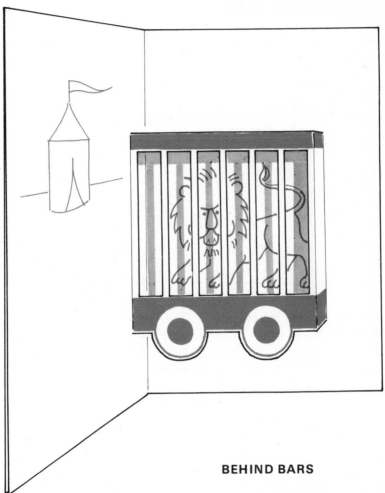

BEHIND BARS

This is a flat-fronted stand-out card of the type diagrammed on the following pages. But in this case bars have been made by cutting holes in front of the cage and a lion has been drawn on the under layer of paper.

FLAT-FRONTED STAND-OUT CLOCK

First fold the top edge to the bottom edge. Crease firmly and open up.

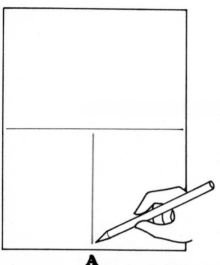

A

1. Draw, *do not fold*, the centre vertical line. Call this line *A*.

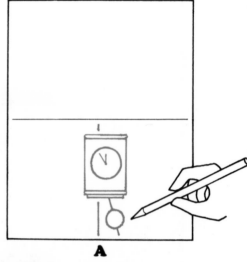

A

2. Draw your design in the lower half. Draw it to one side, but let it overlap the centre vertical line.

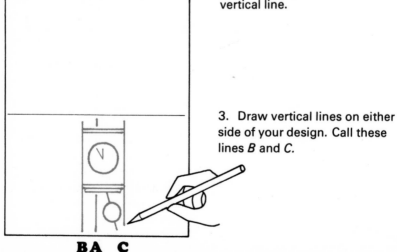

BA C

3. Draw vertical lines on either side of your design. Call these lines *B* and *C*.

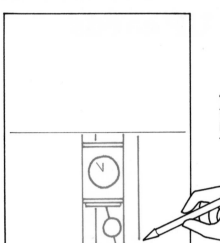

BA CD

4. Now draw a vertical line *D* the same distance to the right of line *C* as line *A* is from line *B*. That is to say, $CD = AB$.

5. Make two cuts between the outermost verticals (lines *B* and *D*) at the top and bottom of your design, or at a suitable place through the design. Take care not to cut beyond lines *B* and *D*.
Then fold the top edge down behind to the bottom edge.

6. Close from left to right, allowing the design to project forward.

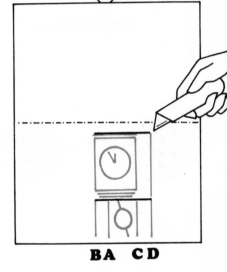

BA CD

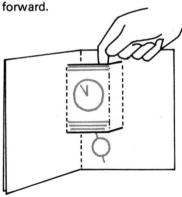

7. Finally, decorate the front of the card.

Classic pop-UP cards

When one of these cards is opened, part of the illustration pops right
up above the top edge of the card.

Many types of subject are suitable for cards constructed in this way,
but it is better if subjects are chosen which have at least some of their
interest at the top, in the part which does the popping-up. The clown,
bunny and circus strongman in the accompanying illustration all have
this in common.

The message itself may be included in the pop-up area. The
strongman's weights, for example, can be used as a background for
greetings.

Minimum materials needed

paper/pencil/knife or scissors

POP-UP CLOWN

Use a rectangle of proportions
about 2 : 1.

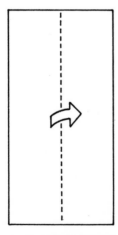

1. Fold in half longways so that
the folded edge is on the left.

2. Bring the top edge over so
that it lies along the right-hand
edge. Make a firm crease.

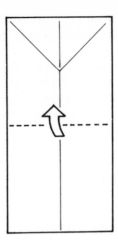

3. Improve the crease made in step 2 by folding backwards and forwards once or twice. Open up.

4. Fold the bottom edge up to the top edge. Turn over.

5. Close the card from left to right, allowing the top edge of the inner layer to project forward.

6. Cut horizontally about one quarter of the way down. Remove the top of the card.

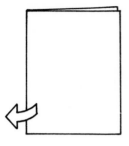

7. Open up.

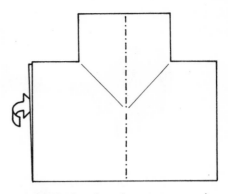

8. Notice that the centre panel pops up when the card is opened. You can draw your design now, making full use of this panel. Or if your design is symmetrical, fold the left edge behind to the right edge . . .

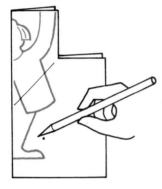

9. . . . and draw half of the design.

10. Cut in from the 'shoulder' of the card until you meet the outline of your design. Then cut around that part of the design which is above the 'shoulder level' of the card.

After completing your design, close the card again as in step 5.

11. Finally, decorate the front of the card.

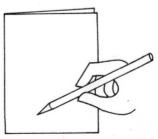

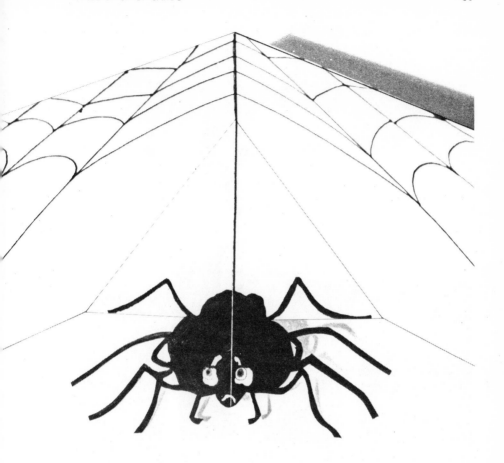

EXTENDED POP-UP CARDS

The action of a pop-up card can be magnified by gluing an extension to the centre panel. Complete steps 1–8 of the classic pop-up card. Then re-fold so that the top edges of the two layers of paper lie together. Make a reverse fold at the top of the centre panel to receive the cut out design.

X-ray view of closed card. When
opened . . .

. . . the skeleton jumps out.

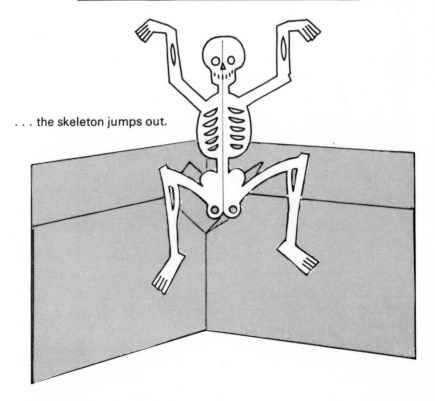

ANIMATED figures

On the next few pages instructions are given for making a card in which a figure raises an arm. This technique can be modified to make arms which descend or legs which lift in a kicking action.

It is surprising how many different meanings can be given to this single raised arm action. An arm may be raised in greeting, or to say, GOODBYE, or to hold up a glass to wish, GOOD LUCK. Whatever message you want to convey should be made clear by the figure you have chosen and the treatment given to it.

The schoolmaster opposite can be used to point at a message, giving the warning, DON'T FORGET . . . The poor man who is raising a revolver to his head might be used in a card sent as an apology for some lapse or indiscretion.

Minimum materials needed

paper/pencil/knife or scissors/ruler

SALUTING POLICEMAN

Fold the top edge to the bottom edge. Make a crease and open up.

1. Draw (do not fold) the vertical centre line. Call this line A. Draw a vertical line B a little to the left of line A.

B A

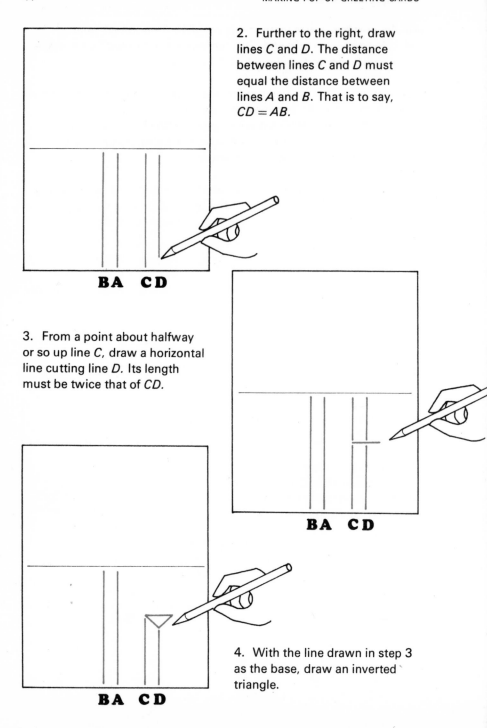

2. Further to the right, draw lines *C* and *D*. The distance between lines *C* and *D* must equal the distance between lines *A* and *B*. That is to say, $CD = AB$.

BA   CD

3. From a point about halfway or so up line *C*, draw a horizontal line cutting line *D*. Its length must be twice that of *CD*.

BA   CD

BA   CD

4. With the line drawn in step 3 as the base, draw an inverted triangle.

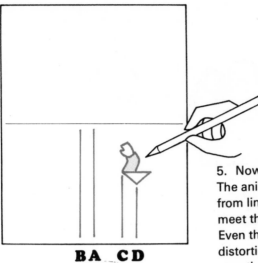

BA CD

5. Now start to draw the figure. The animated arm must 'grow' from lines C and D where they meet the base of the triangle. Even though it may mean distorting your figure, make sure that the arm grows from the base of the triangle between lines C and D exactly.

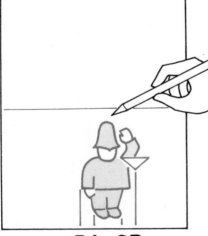

BA CD

6. Complete your drawing. It is convenient but not essential to place the static arm between lines A and B, and the legs between lines A and C.

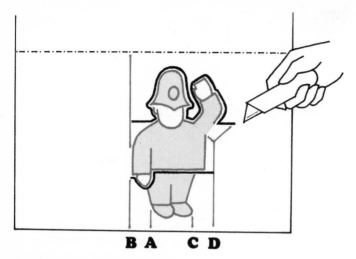

B A   C D

7. Make a cut from line *B* around the top of the figure to line *D*, and then continue the cut along the base of the triangle.

Make a lower cut, at a convenient place, from line *B* to line *D*.

Fold the top edge down behind to the bottom edge.

8. Bring the body forward and the arm down, folding along the lines as shown, and close the card from left to right.

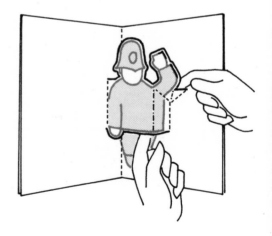

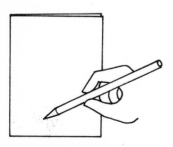

9. Finally, decorate the front of the card.

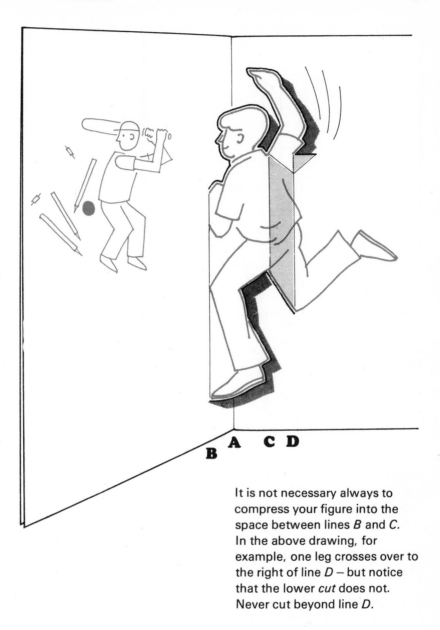

B A C D

It is not necessary always to
compress your figure into the
space between lines *B* and *C*.
In the above drawing, for
example, one leg crosses over to
the right of line *D* — but notice
that the lower *cut* does not.
Never cut beyond line *D*.

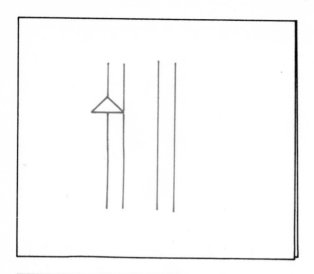

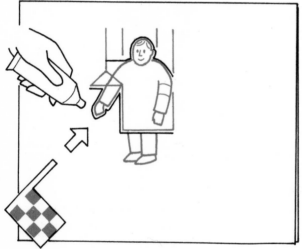

HURRAH ! YOU'VE COME FIRST

It is possible to give the arm a downward-moving action simply by turning the triangle drawn in step 4 upside down. The arm *must* cut the base line of the triangle between lines *C* and *D*.

The chequered flag is made separately and glued to the official's hand.

More animated figures

The type of card shown in the foregoing illustration is rather
similar in construction to the opening flower described at the
beginning of this book. The figures open their arms in a gesture which
can be given different meanings according to the type of figure
employed and the accompanying message.

For example, the clergyman is seen to be giving a blessing. The young
woman is saying, COME BACK. ALL IS FORGIVEN. Were the figure of
an angler to be used, he would appear to be demonstrating the size of
'the one that got away'. Other figures might be made to shrug their
shoulders in resignation or lift their arms to show off the size of their
muscles.

Take care in step 3 when drawing the arm. Do not place the armpit
too close to the upper diagonal crease. If possible, continue the outline
of the figure from the arm down to the lower diagonal crease.

Minimum materials needed

paper/pencil/knife or scissors

BLESS YOU !

Use a 2 : 1 rectangle.

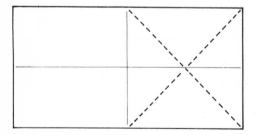

First make the centre creases by
folding the edges together and
opening up.

1. Make diagonal creases in the
right-hand square.

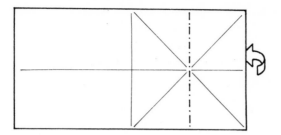

2. Fold the right edge behind to
the centre crease.

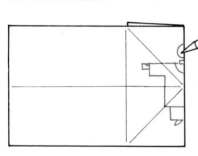

3. With the folded edge as the
centre line, draw half a figure.
Place the arm in the area
between the two diagonals.

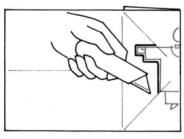

4. Through the two layers of
paper, cut around your design
between the diagonals only.
Then open up.

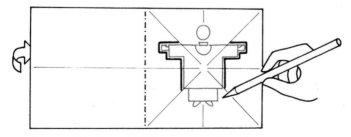

5. Complete your design.
Fold the left edge behind to the
right edge.

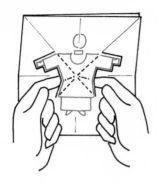

6. Close the card from top to bottom, bringing the arms forward and down as shown.

7. Finally, decorate the front of the card.

Decorative FAN action

These cards employ strips of pleated paper which open in the same way as a fan. The ruff of the choirboy has been glued horizontally to the two inside faces of the card. His head has been constructed using the simple stand-out technique. The Spanish lady's skirt is made from three strips of pleated paper stuck diagonally instead of horizontally.

The pleated strips should be made from thin paper. Flint paper (glossy) or surface paper (matt) is suitable as are some of the brightly-coloured papers now available as stationery.

Instead of drawing or painting your design around the pleated strip, you may prefer to treat the whole thing as a collage and incorporate the pleated strip into an illustration made from cut-out areas of coloured or patterned paper.

Minimum materials needed

paper/pencil (or gummed coloured paper)/knife or scissors/glue

BALLET DANCER

1. Fold the left edge to the right edge. Make the centre crease and open up.

2. Cut a separate piece of thinner paper into a strip proportioned about 1 : 5.

Pleat this into sixteenths. This can be done by first folding the strip in half, then into quarters, then into eighths and finally into sixteenths.

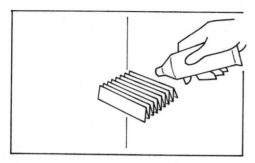

3. Stick one end of the pleated
strip to the card horizontally,
just to the right of the centre
line.

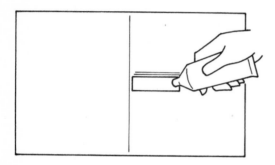

4. Apply adhesive to the top
panel of the pleated strip.

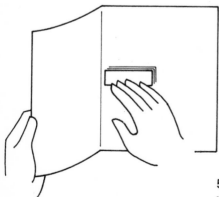

5. Close the card. Hold the
pleated strip down as you do so.

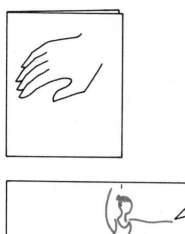

6. Press firmly so that the pleated strip will stick to the top layer of card. Allow a little time for it to dry.

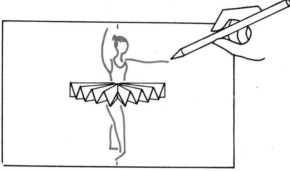

7. Now open the card. The strip will spread out like a fan. Draw your design and close the card.

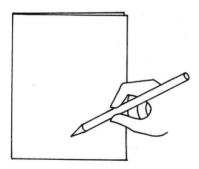

8. Finally, decorate the cover.

Pop-*through* cards

This type of card has a picture on the front which will *re-appear inside* when the card is opened. It can be used to show your subject against two different backgrounds or in two different kinds of situation.

For example, a person might be shown in familiar surroundings on the front of the card, but when it is opened, the same person could be made to appear immediately in a foreign country or in another period of history.

You can make good use of this 'before and after' effect in constructing cards to celebrate such occasions as marriage, change of occupation or success in examinations, because they provide opportunities of showing two situations; one in which the person for whom the card is intended (bride, new employee, etc.) appears now and one in which he might appear in the future.

If you can draw good likenesses of your friends, you will be able to show them in amusing situations.

Minimum materials needed

paper/pencil/knife or scissors/ruler

RAIN . . . OR SHINE . . .

A pop-through card in which the same figure appears against two contrasting backgrounds.

Start with a rectangle of paper. Fold it in half widthways. Make sure the folded edge is at the top.

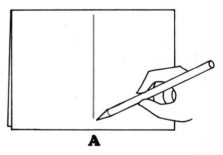

1. Draw (do not fold) the centre vertical line. Call this line *A*.

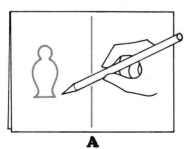

2. Draw your design on the left. Keep it simple and symmetrical.

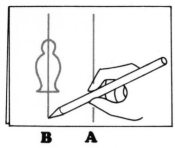

B   A

3. Find the centre of your design and draw a vertical line through it. Call this line *B*.

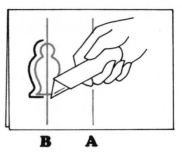

B   A

4. Through the two layers of paper, cut around the outline of your design on the left-hand side of line *B* only. Then open up.

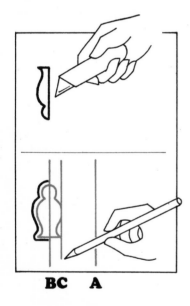

BC   A

5. In the upper half, make a vertical cut between the two ends of the outline cut made in step 4. Remove the surplus paper.

In the lower half, draw a vertical line just to the right of your design. Call this line *C*.

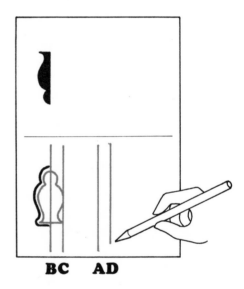

BC   AD

6. Draw a vertical line *D* the same distance to the right of line *A* as line *C* is from line *B*. That is to say, $AD = BC$.

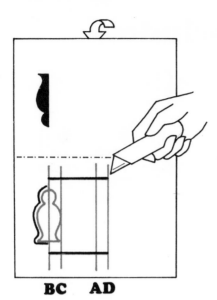

BC   AD

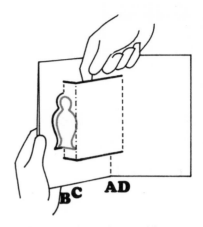

7. First cut horizontal lines above and below your design from line *B* to line *D*. Then fold the top edge down behind to the bottom edge.

8. Start to close the card from left to right. Bring the centre part forward making creases as shown. Your design will protrude through the hole cut in the under layer. Close the card completely.

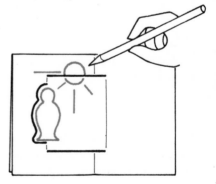

9. Now the design will lie flat against the front of the card. Draw a background.

10. Open and draw a contrasting background for the figure which has re-appeared inside the card.

Face-at-the-window cards

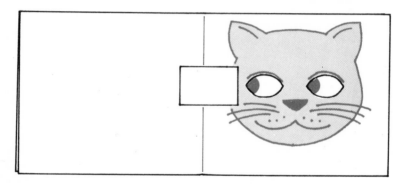

FACE-AT-THE-WINDOW
technique employed to make
eyes which swivel from one side
to the other.

This type of card employs a strip which moves between the two layers
of paper. Whatever is drawn on the strip can be seen through an area
which has been cut out of the design.

A face can be made to appear at a window by cutting out a rectangular
shape for the window and drawing a face on the strip. The face need
not appear from the side because the same action can be used where
the design moves upwards or downwards. The head of a fireman, for
example, could be made to appear at a window from below as if he
were climbing a ladder; Father Christmas might show himself *down* a
chimney.

The same technique can be employed to make faces with eyes which
swivel from one side to the other. Ways of developing this are shown
on the following pages.

In constructing these, take care that the distance between lines *A* and
C is not less than one-and-a-half times the distance between lines *A*
and *B*. If *AC* is too short there is a danger that the strip will buckle
when the card is closed. Let us say that *AC* must be not less than one-
and-a-half times *AB* and not more than twice *AB*.

Minimum materials needed

paper/pencil/knife or scissors/ruler/glue

I'VE GOT MY EYE ON YOU

First fold the sides of your
rectangle together and make
creases to find the centre lines.
Open up.

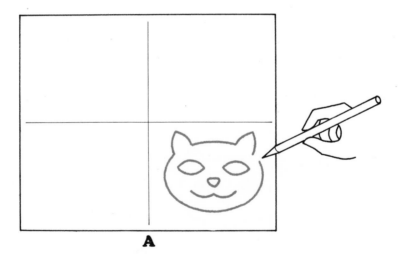

A

1. Draw your design in one
quarter. The part to be cut out
(in this case the eyes) should not
be placed too near the vertical
centre line *A*.

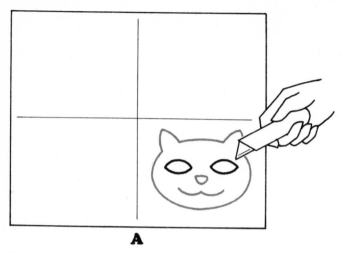

A

2. Cut out that part of your design which is to be removed.

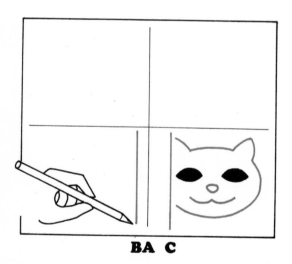

BA C

3. Draw a vertical line *B* to the left of centre line *A*. The distance *AB* should equal half the distance you intend your animated design to travel (which in this case means half the width of an eye). Then draw line *C* between line *A* and the cut out area. *AC* should be almost twice the distance of *AB*.

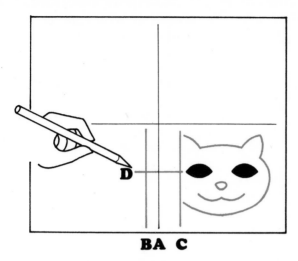

BA C

4. Draw a horizontal line *D*
across lines *A*, *B* and *C*, centred
on the cut out area.

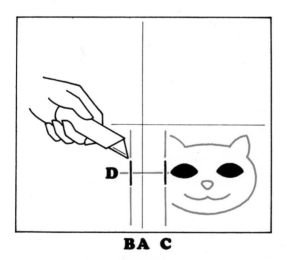

BA C

5. With line *D* as the centre, cut
slits in lines *B* and *C* a little
wider than the cut out area.

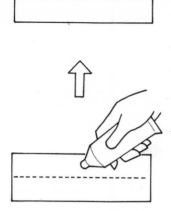

6. Now cut a strip of paper for the lever mechanism. This should be twice as wide as the slits cut in step 5. Fold in half and glue.

Its length should be about equal to the distance between line *B* and the right-hand edge of the card.

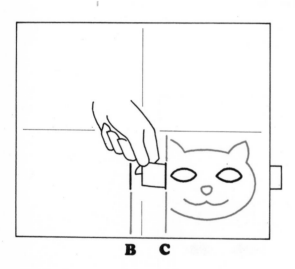

B   C

7. Thread this strip through the slits in lines *B* and *C*. Turn over.

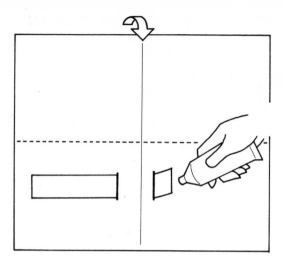

8. Make sure that the strip completely covers the cut out area. Then lift the right-hand end and stick it in place.

Fold the top edge of the card down to the bottom edge.

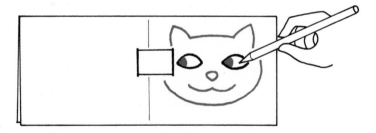

9. Continue your design on the strip through the cut out area. Remember, when your card is in the open position your drawing should show the completed action.

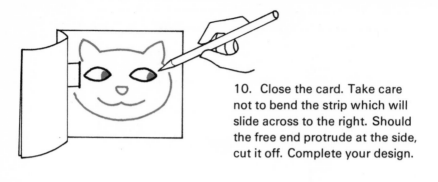

10. Close the card. Take care not to bend the strip which will slide across to the right. Should the free end protrude at the side, cut it off. Complete your design.

11. Finally, decorate the front of the card.

SLEEPING BEAUTY

Sleeping Beauty opens her eyes when the card is opened.

This card is made in exactly the same way as the one diagrammed in this section, except that two strips are used for the mechanism.

An interesting feature is that the *eyelashes* of the closed eyes becomes *eyebrows* when the eyes are opened.

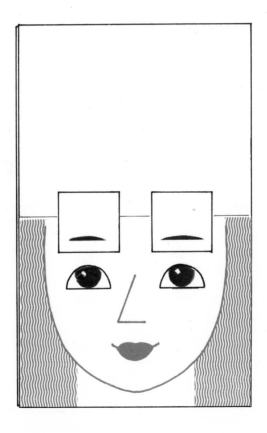

Here is a card with a double action. As the girl swivels her eyes she also licks her ice-cream.

This card too is made on the same principle as the one shown in this section. But a 'tongue' has been pinned to the strip mechanism with a paper fastener and then passed through a slit in the mouth.

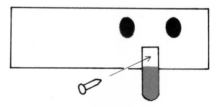

Notice that the strip has been made extra wide to allow space for fastening the tongue. The slit in the mouth is only just wide enough to allow the tongue to pass through.

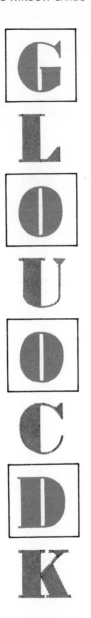

GOOD LUCK

The face-at-the-window technique can be employed with short messages too. Here the letters G-O-O-D are framed in four square holes. These will slide up to reveal the letters L-U-C-K. It is not necessary for both words to have the same number of letters. Squares can be left blank.

Pop-across cards

The boy pops across and kisses
the girl on the cheek.

In construction, these are very similar to face-at-the-window cards,
but in this case the strip mechanism is used as a support to which part
of the design is attached. This part will become animated when the
card is opened and move across from one side to the other.

The animated part of the design can be quite large and irregular in
shape provided that the base (XY in the diagrams) is made narrow. The
base has to fit into a slit and yet leave plenty of free space in the slit so
that it can move along.

Minimum materials needed

paper/pencil/knife or scissors/ruler/glue

First fold the sides of your rectangle together, make the centre creases and open up.

Call the centre horizontal line *A*.

1. Draw line *B* above line *A*. Draw line *C* at almost twice this distance below line *A*. That is to say, *AC* should be almost twice *AB*.

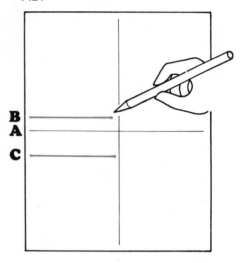

2. Prepare the animated part of your design on separate paper. *XY* is the base of the design where it will meet the background.

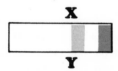

That part to the right of *XY* will be visible in the finished card. The paper to the left of *XY* will be used to attach the design to the support strip at a later stage.

3. Draw a vertical line, crossing lines *B*, *A* and *C*, down to the bottom edge. Call this line *D*.

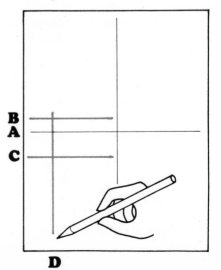

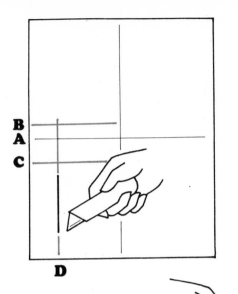

4. Now, starting a little below line *C*, cut a slit in line *D*. Its length should equal twice *AC* plus the width of the base *XY*. That is to say, the length of the slit should be $2AC + XY$.

5. Starting at line *D*, cut slits of equal length in lines *B* and *C*.

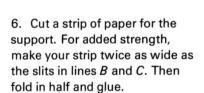

6. Cut a strip of paper for the support. For added strength, make your strip twice as wide as the slits in lines *B* and *C*. Then fold in half and glue.

Its length should be about equal to the distance from line *B* to the bottom edge of the card. Any surplus can be cut off after the card is completed.

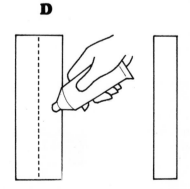

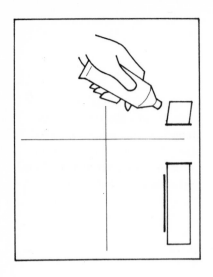

7. Turn over. Thread the strip through the slits in lines *B* and *C*. Stick the top end to the card.

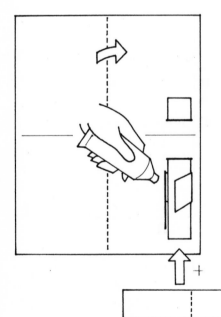

8. Thread the animated part of your design through the vertical slit. Slide it up as far as it will go. Make sure that *XY* is lying along line *D*. Then stick to the support strip.

When dry, fold the left edge of the card to the right edge.

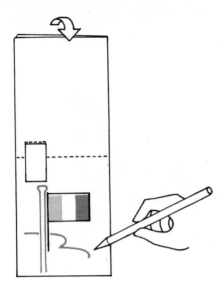

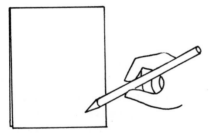

9. Complete your design. Close from top to bottom, taking care not to bend the strip but letting it slide downwards.

Should the free end of the strip protrude when the card is closed, cut it off.

10. Finally, decorate the front of the card.

KEEP ON TRYING!

The animated part of pop-across cards can be quite large and irregular in shape provided that the base *XY* is made comparatively narrow.

But note that the card must be sufficiently wide to accommodate the figure when it is in the closed position. The card illustrated here is *not* wide enough. When *XY* moves to the right-hand end of the slit, the legs will stick out at the side.

Intertwined hearts

Young people were making intricately woven pairs of hearts to send to their valentines long before there was a greeting card industry. Because they are fun to make and yet, despite their long history, not widely known, instructions for making them are included in this book even though they are not 'moveables'.

Any number of cuts can be made and the angled strips can be intertwined in ways other than the one shown here. No doubt you will want to discover for yourself what patterns will appear by weaving the hearts together in various ways.

In step 4 it is necessary to make cuts at an angle of 45 degrees.

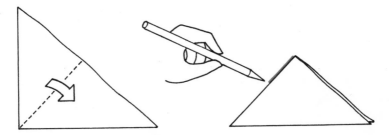

To make a 45 degree angle without a set square, take the corner of a scrap of paper and fold the two straight edges together.

Minimum materials needed

coloured paper (two sheets)/pencil/knife or scissors/ruler

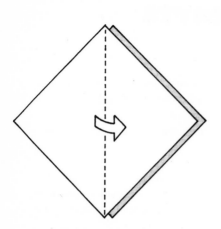

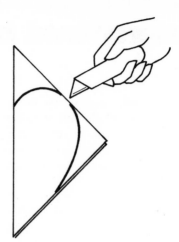

1. Place two squares of equal size together and fold them in half diagonally.

2. Cut a full rounded curve, starting from the folded edge.

3. Draw a vertical line, more or less in the centre.

4. Now make a series of cuts from the folded edge to the vertical line drawn in step 3. The cuts should be equidistant and at an angle of 45 degrees.

Then open up and separate the two hearts.

5. Turn one heart upside down. Thread the point marked *X* through the topmost slit of the coloured heart. Then, working your way downwards, thread each of the remaining white points through its opposite slit in the coloured heart.

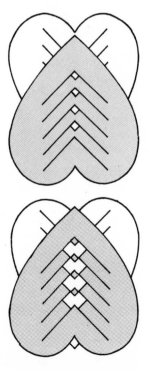

6. This is the result of step 5.

Gently move the hearts a little closer so that more and more of the white points become visible. When point *X* has passed over the second slit, find and raise the coloured point under it. Tuck point *X* under this coloured point. Tuck each of the remaining white points under its opposite coloured point.

7. This shows step 6 completed.

Continue to move the hearts closer together, gradually intertwining them in this way.

You will discover other patterns
by weaving the angled strips in
various ways.

Making a pop-UP book

Now that you have learnt these techniques, perhaps you would like to use them to make a complete pop-up book of your own.

Instructions follow for making a small book which can accommodate eight pop-up scenes — quite sufficient to start with. If you do want to add more scenes later, this can be done by making them separately in the same way as greeting cards and joining them to the other pages with gummed paper as shown in steps 4 and 5.

PLANNING THE BOOK

Choose a well-known fairy tale or nursery rhyme.

Break it up into 6 to 8 scenes.

Make a list of the different types of action you could *possibly* use in each scene.

Then decide on which of these you will use. Try to include as many different kinds of action as you can. You can always have a stand-out scene when nothing else seems suitable.

Minimum materials needed

paper/Manilla (or similar card)/pencil/knife or scissors/ruler/glue/gummed paper strip

MAKING A POP-UP BOOK

1. Cut a sheet of paper of Imperial (22" × 30"—60 × 76 cm) or similar size in two lengthways.

Then fold each of the halves in two lengthways.

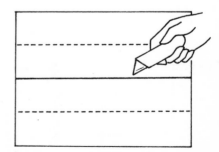

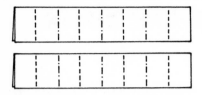

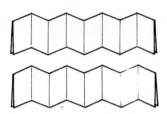

2. Pleat each of the strips into eighths.

3. You now have eight double pages. Draw your illustrations and construct your pop-up actions on these. Remember to unfold the under layer of paper before making cuts.

When you have completed your illustrations, prepare to join the two sections together.

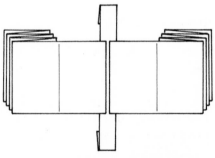

4. First take a strip of gummed paper (preferably white) sticky side up. Fold both ends under and stick these to the table.

5. Stick the centre pages to the gummed strip. Leave a little space between the two sections.

Turn over and repeat steps 4 and 5.

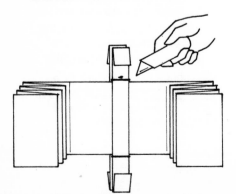

6. Trim off the ends of the gummed paper and repleat the centre pages . . .

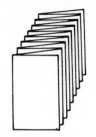

7. . . . like this.

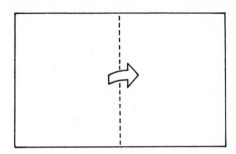

8. For the cover, cut a rectangle of card (e.g. Manilla). Its width should be three times that of a single page and its height an inch or so more.

Fold it in half widthways.

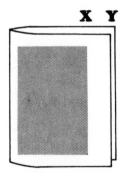

X Y

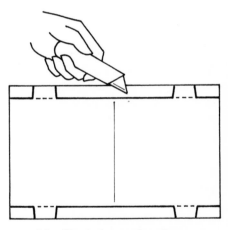

9. Place the pleated strip inside the cover as close to the fold as it will go. As this X-ray view shows, the strip, because of its thickness, will not go right up against the fold.

Note the distance between the right-hand edges of the pleated strip and the right-hand edges of the cover. Call this distance *XY*.

10. Open the card and remove the pleated strip. Cut away the top and bottom edges of the card so that its height equals the height of the pages. At a distance from each corner equal to *XY*, leave tabs whose width should also equal *XY*.

Fold these tabs forward and flatten.

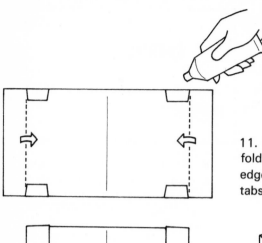

11. Glue the four tabs. Then fold the left- and right-hand edges forward and stick to the tabs.

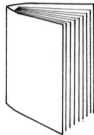

12. You now have a jacket for the pleated strip of pages. Tuck the first and last pages into the left and right pockets of the jacket and close.

13. The completed pop-up book.

Elgan Jones's
Pop-OPEN gift box

Elgan Jones has devised several versions of his ingenious box, but the one described here is probably the easiest for you to make.

It works in this way: move the coloured band downwards and the four lid flaps spring open in a delightful and quite unexpected way.

Pop-open boxes make attractive containers for gifts, but no doubt you will want to make at least one to keep for yourself. Both hobbyists and housewives will find them useful for storing their bits and pieces. A set of these boxes, made from paper of carefully chosen design, can look well on a dressing-table or kitchen shelf.

As containers for sweets and biscuits, pop-open boxes are sure to give pleasure when passed around at parties.

Minimum materials needed

square-sided box/paper or thin card/pencil/knife or scissors/ruler/glue/gummed paper strip

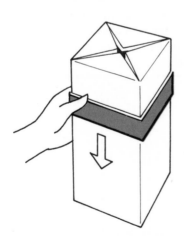 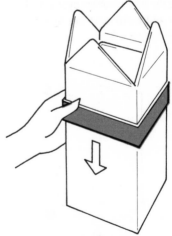

Take hold of the coloured band and move it downwards gently . . .

. . . The four lid flaps will spring open. Continue to pull downwards . . .

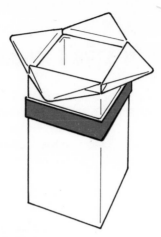

. . . and the lid will spread out
into an attractive star pattern.

POP-OPEN GIFT BOX

1. Take a square-sided tin or
cardboard box or something
similar. Measure the width and
height of one of its sides. Call
the width AB and the height
BC.

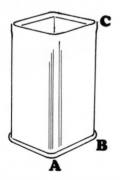

2. Now cut a sheet of paper or
thin card into a rectangle whose
width equals four times AB, and
whose length equals BC plus
twice AB.

Divide the width into quarters.
Fold the two top corners down
so that they lie on the centre
line.

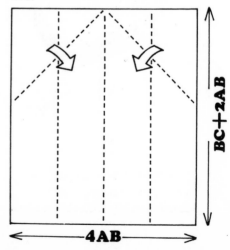

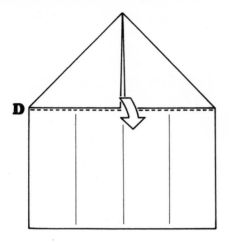

3. By folding forward, make a firm crease along the horizontal edge. Call this line *D.* Unfold.

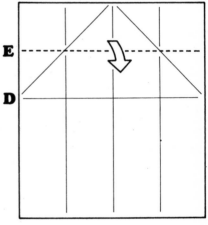

4. Fold the top edge down to line *D* and crease. Call this line *E.* Unfold.

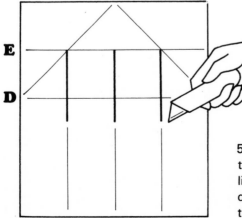

5. Make vertical cuts in each of the three quarter lines. Start at line *E* and cut downwards for a distance equal to one-and-a-half times *DE.*

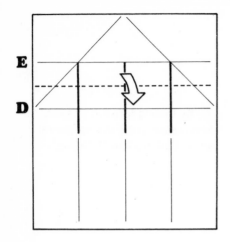

6. Fold the top edge down so that line *E* lies on line *D*.

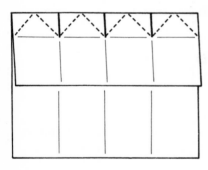

7. Fold the upper corners of the four 'teeth' down so that they lie on line *E*. Fold them backwards and forwards once or twice to make sharp creases.

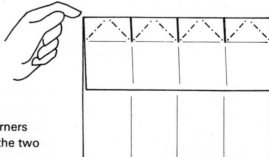

8. Now push these corners down and in between the two layers.

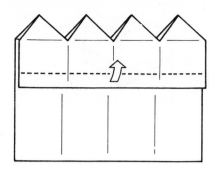

9. Fold up the front edge. Turn over.

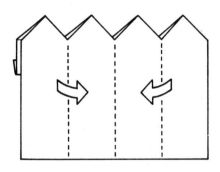

10. Raise the sides by folding on the quarter lines . . .

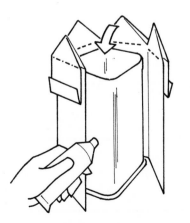

11. . . . and stick neatly and firmly to the box. Then push the four triangular flaps into a horizontal position.

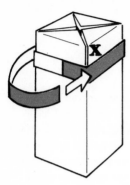

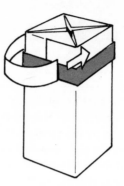

12. Wrap a strip of coloured paper around the raised edge and stick down.

Notice the place marked *X* where two raw edges meet . . .

13. . . . Strengthen the box by sticking a strip of paper around here too.

Your box is now completed and ready for use.

Historical Notes

The custom of sending greeting cards began in the latter half of the eighteenth century with the sending of valentines. They were generally made by the senders themselves and were often elaborately decorated. In the eighteen-forties a type of valentine which was the forerunner of more complex pop-ups appeared. The illustration in this type of card incorporated a flap which could be lifted to reveal what lay behind. Scenes of churchyards, the church having doors which opened to reveal a bride and groom, were very popular.

After the invention of cheap and easy colour reproduction processes in the eighteen-sixties, the custom of sending greeting cards became much more widespread and Christmas overtook St Valentine's day in importance.

In the eighteen-seventies, cards and books which contained scenes like stage settings were produced in Germany. They were formed from several layers of card which could be pulled up to make a foreground, middle distance and background. Germany and neighbouring central European countries remained the source of all the most inventive novelty cards for a very long time. It was here, in the last decade of the nineteenth century that true pop-ups were produced. These cards contained illustrations which stood up automatically when opened without the need for pulling a tab.

There was a revival of interest in pop-up cards during the nineteen-thirties which died down in the second world war. After the war a new type of book was produced in Czechoslovakia. The mechanism was controlled by interlocking strips of card which worked together so that several movements could be incorporated into one scene.

In the nineteen-sixties the present revival of interest began and pop-up techniques were employed in advertising material and record sleeves. Some remarkable outsize pop-up cards and many bright and colourful pop-up books from Japan are to be seen in the shops today.